DR. MYLES

KEYS *for* CHANGE

W

WHITAKER
HOUSE

Unless otherwise indicated, Scripture quotations are taken from the *Holy Bible, New International Version*®, NIV®, © 1973, 1978, 1984 by the International Bible Society. Used by permission of Zondervan. All rights reserved. Scripture quotations marked (NKJV) are taken from the *New King James Version*, © 1979, 1980, 1982, 1984 by Thomas Nelson, Inc. Used by permission.

KEYS FOR CHANGE

ISBN: 978-1-60374-151-4
Printed in the United States of America
© 2009 by Dr. Myles Munroe

Dr. Myles Munroe
Bahamas Faith Ministries International
P.O. Box N9583
Nassau, Bahamas
E-mail: bfmadmin@bfmmm.com
www.bfmmm.com; www.bfmi.tv; www.mylesmunroe.tv

Whitaker House
1030 Hunt Valley Circle
New Kensington, PA 15068
www.whitakerhouse.com

No part of this book may be reproduced or transmitted in any form or by any means, electronic or mechanical—including photocopying, recording, or by any information storage and retrieval system—without permission in writing from the publisher. Please direct your inquiries to permissionseditor@whitakerhouse.com.

1 2 3 4 5 6 7 8 9 10 11 12 ᲚᲘ 17 16 15 14 13 12 11 10 09

INTRODUCTION

*N*o matter who or where you are—regardless of your country, race, ethnicity, language, and disposition—time and change will affect you. Life is continually handing us personal, family, community, and national changes.

You may feel more trepidation than trust regarding the inevitability of change. Yet you can learn to embrace change with a positive attitude and use it to benefit your life, as well as others' lives.

Or, perhaps you anticipate change in the future and are excited about it. You can come to view times of transition with an expanded perspective, discovering tremendous opportunities for personal, professional, and corporate growth. These new possibilities hold an exciting future for you.

Regardless of your current attitude toward transitions, *Keys for Change* will help you to understand the nature and role of change in your life. As you consider these principles and insights about change, you will develop the faith and courage to embrace the next season of your life. Responding effectively to inevitable change and implementing desired change is the path to fulfilling your God-given potential—and your unique contribution to your generation.

—*Dr. Myles Munroe*

Change is one of the most important factors in human life, whether that change is imposed on us or we've created the change ourselves and are eagerly anticipating its possibilities. Yet most people don't manage change effectively and positively.

*H*ow we relate to change has a significant impact on our quality of life and whether or not we accomplish what we are meant to during our time on earth.

Understanding how to view, respond to, and benefit from change is vital to a well-balanced and fulfilling life.

$\mathcal{G}$od is the original Innovator who initiated the principle of change on earth by creating time and seasons. *"God said, 'Let there be lights in the expanse of the sky…, and let them serve as signs to mark seasons and days and years'"* (Genesis 1:14). Our world functions in time because God created it that way.

$\mathcal{N}$atural rhythms exist all around us. There are seasons in nature, with corresponding changes in the weather, and seasons in our bodies. There are seasons in our personal lives and seasons within the changing tides of human history. The very nature of seasons implies change.

$\mathscr{S}$ome of the change we experience is a result of evil acts perpetrated by others. Sin entered the world when humanity rebelled against God and went its own way. Yet change itself is not a result of the fall of humanity. It is built into creation.

There is a time for everything, and a season for every activity under heaven" (Ecclesiastes 3:1). One of God's promises is that everything on earth is only for a season. This truth may be called the "promise paradox."

$\mathcal{F}$ive foundational principles of change are (1) *nothing on earth is as permanent as change*, (2) *change is continual*, (3) *everything changes*, (4) *change is inevitable*, and (5) *change is a principle of life and creation.*

*W*henever you encounter change—
especially change you consider disruptive
or distressing—don't feel you're all alone in
this. We are all subject to change!

Change is a human "equalizer." It is every human being's experience. If you think things aren't changing, just wait a week or a month or a year. Nationality, race, ethnicity, language, disposition, wealth, youth, talent, intelligence, popularity, success, ambition, or good intentions don't make you immune: no matter who you are, you will experience change.

Change is the essence of our experience of life. Seasons can be physical, mental, emotional, spiritual, or societal. The word *season* is often used to define change that is not a short-term event but rather an extended period of transition. Seasons involve the replacement of one environment or condition with another.

*W*e experience four distinct types of change in life: (1) change that happens *to us*, (2) change that happens *around us*, (3) change that happens *within us*, and (4) change that *we initiate*.

Change that happens *to us* affects our personal lives, families, and careers. Change that happens *around us* affects our society, nation, or world but also has some impact on us personally.

Change that happens *within us* affects who we are physically, emotionally, mentally, or spiritually. Change that *we initiate* is created or altered by plans we implement to move us from the present to a preferred future.

$\mathcal{C}$hange transports the present into
a future that demands a response.

The average person doesn't *respond* to change—he *reacts* to it. Reacting means having a negative attitude toward change—anxiety, fear, desperation, anger—or taking an action against change before really thinking about it or its consequences. Merely *reacting* to change essentially gives change the advantage over you, rendering you a victim of your circumstances.

To deny change means to insist on continuing business as usual—when it's no longer usual.

Change is always the introduction of the future to the present. Change is tomorrow taking over today, and a denial of change is a decision to live in yesterday. Eventually, to deny change is to become irrelevant.

*I*t's not healthy to believe that life will always remain the same. Everything may be stable now, but there will be a transition or point of stress in the future. Most of life's disappointments and stresses come from our trying to keep things the way they are or expecting them to stay the way they are.

Some people end up sacrificing their lives to their lost pasts. They lose out on opportunities to enjoy the relationships they still have, to meet new friends, to expand their knowledge, and to explore the uncharted territories of their true potentials—all for the sake of trying to protect the way life used to be.

If we *know* that everything in life is only for a season—and this has to be an individual revelation for each person— then it takes some of the shock out of life when we experience situations that otherwise would lead us to grief, disappointment, or fear.

*N*o matter the source of change—be it personal, social, political, economic, or spiritual—we can't pretend that the change is not happening. Pretending has no effect on change. Seek to understand change, accept its reality, and commit to fulfilling the new role it demands from you.

KEYS for CHANGE

The only way for you to move forward to where you want to go in life, regardless of your circumstances, is to initiate desired change and to address unwanted change constructively.

*I*n general, think of change as your friend rather than your enemy. Change is not the kind of "friend" who will sit and commiserate with you at a pity party but a friend who will encourage you to be the best you can be. See change as the arrival of opportunity rather than an invasion of destruction.

When change occurs, seek to understand the value of both your past and present roles. Each of us is important to the Creator's great program of purpose in this world, and His purposes continue, even though circumstances and people change.

*I*f you react, you are a victim.
If you respond, you are a victor.

*I*f you react, change leads your life. If you respond, *you* lead change in your life.

*K*nowing how to respond to inevitable change rather than just reacting to it can keep you at peace during any change you may experience. Responding rather than reacting to change also enables you to grow stronger for the next phase of your life.

If you are to engage fully in life, then you must not ignore the truth about the future. It holds one of two options for you: respond effectively to change or be a victim of change. *You have the power to determine the quality and effectiveness of your future by your response to change.*

*I*ntegrating yourself in change doesn't necessarily mean that you support it. You understand that it is a reality and position yourself to move forward in life in the midst of it. If you do support it, you actively seek to help the change to take place. You embrace it and search for your place in it.

We can become a part of God's process, which always works for our good when we are aligned with His purposes. (See Romans 8:28.) When we are in step with His plans, we can have confidence in any situation, however unsettling.

*W*e can't fight change when God's hand is truly in it. When God-ordained change occurs, you don't want to *let* change happen—you want to *help* change happen. Those who survive and benefit in the midst of change understand their places in the process and participate fully in what the change was intended to deliver.

Change will happen either with us or without us. We can be tempted to withdraw from active participation in God's purposes as a way of expressing our dissatisfaction with His will. This dangerous attitude says, "If I am not in charge and in control, then I will not get involved."

*T*hose who prepare and plan for change are never really surprised by it because they understand that change is integral to life.

*O*ur safeguard against the detrimental effects of unprepared-for events and circumstances is to continually *expect* change to occur in all areas of life. Grasping just this one truth will prepare you to handle many of the challenges that accompany change.

A constructive response to the inevitability of change is to prepare your mind, your emotions, your family, your finances, and so forth for a number of eventualities. Prepare yourself not only for what you *want* to happen but also for what *could* happen.

$\mathcal{B}$y planning and preparing for change, you reduce stress and fear, gain greater control over your circumstances and environment, increase your confidence, and make change your servant. This is the essence of *response to change*, as opposed to *reaction to change*, because it requires forethought.

*A*void becoming unsettled, anxious, or angry about change by expecting it and always having a contingency plan. If there is nothing you can do to prevent a certain situation, put a plan into action to turn it to your advantage. Always think in terms of restructuring your situation to help you further your goals.

KEYS for CHANGE

Initiating change means realizing its potential and power and actively creating it to further your vision and goals for your life based on your purpose.

$\mathcal{T}$o initiate change means that you (1) determine what changes in your life and environment will best serve the purposes you have been called to fulfill on this earth and (2) order your life and environment according to these best interests.

All change will cost something, even if it's just the loss of the familiar. We must be willing to let go of what *isn't* working for us in order to pursue what is best for us. Are you willing to let go of the past and become proactive about the future? If so, you are ready to become a world changer.

*J*ust as every product has a shelf life, the present has a "shelf life." The way you currently think and what you're currently doing will change over time, at least to some degree. If they don't, you're not growing and maturing as a person!

$\mathcal{M}$any people are "offended" in life by their circumstances and by those whom they blame for those circumstances. Yet taking offense is damaging to a person's spirit. The principle of change assures us that good times won't continue forever, and we must be prepared to avoid the trap of offense.

You can't base your personal value on anything you possess. If you do, then you will lose your value when you no longer possess it. In essence, the effects of change will be able to reduce you to nothing.

You may be expecting too much from other people—or even from yourself. While we want to conduct our lives with excellence, we can't control everything, and we shouldn't try to. Trying to control everything that happens to you will overload your body with stress.

$\mathscr{G}$od won't allow anything to come into your life that you cannot rise above with His help.

Keys for Change

Critical change refers to a traumatic life event, a turning point that completely changes one's way of life, a radical shift in personal or professional status, a dire situation that needs to be addressed, an acute challenge to the status quo, or a "zero hour" when a decision or change *must* be made.

Critical change includes both a disruption and a reordering of people's lives. It impels them to deal with new relationships, issues, environments, and circumstances.

Critical change can be the greatest motivator for progress. Periods of personal, community, or national challenge can be times when we undergo the greatest development in maturity, wisdom, compassion for others, social advancement, and economic development—if we allow the change to stretch us and to exercise our innovative qualities.

53

*L*et your personal motto during times of critical change be "innovation." Learn to use every situation to maximize your growth and creativity and to cause you to think beyond the norm so that you can progress in significant ways.

*I*t is has been said that people initiate personal change only when the pain of remaining the same exceeds the pain of change.

*I*t is comfort that creates *tradition*. It is discomfort that creates *transformation*. The average person doesn't know what he or she is capable of until change affects him or her. In general, the human spirit thrives on finding solutions to chaotic conditions.

*E*agles are the only birds that fly *toward* storms. They spread their wings and use the abnormal wind currents formed by storms in order to soar—giving them an opportunity to rest. They know how to benefit from critical change in their environments. Have you learned the same?

We can become so enamored of what we have already completed that we cease to pursue what we can still accomplish. Change has a way of making us move beyond what used to impress us about ourselves. It shortens our self-congratulatory celebrations and spurs us on to do greater things.

KEYS for CHANGE

*R*eleasing one's potential usually requires the element of responsibility. Another way of saying this is that *ability* requires *responsibility* in order to be manifested. A change in conditions often forces us to accept duties and obligations that make us dig deeper into the reserves in our capacities.

When an unexpected event or situation occurs, it can prompt you to manifest a self that people didn't know was in you—that *you* never knew was in you. Unexpected change can help to manifest who you really are.

*I*n times of change, we must have an element in our lives that is permanent and stable—that transcends past, present, and future. This constant enables us to stay grounded in who we are, where we're going, and the values by which we conduct our lives. Our one constant in change is our Creator God.

*D*espite the fact that everything on earth changes, God declares, *"I the LORD do not change"* (Malachi 3:6). The Creator never changes, in the sense that He is invariable in His nature, character, and integrity. His acts may change, but His essential ways never change. This truth gives us confidence in the midst of unsettling times.

God is not only unchangeable, but He is also eternal. Eternity is not ruled by time. God exists outside of time, although He interacts with human beings and human affairs within the realm of time.

God is the same yesterday, today, and forever. (See Hebrews 13:8.) We can put no real confidence in anything else, for nothing and no one besides God is completely trustworthy and reliable. The greatest security against the disorientation and disruptions of change is reliance on the unchanging God.

*O*ur Creator made us, and He is faithful in all His promises. No matter what changes may come your way, you can depend on Him to fulfill what He has promised.

God keeps His Word. He tells us how things are. He comforts us, but He doesn't give us false promises. He's Someone whom we can count on completely to tell us the truth and to prepare us to handle it.

KEYS for CHANGE

Some people believe that because God doesn't change, He won't do anything different from what they've already seen Him do. When He brings or allows change in their lives to further His purposes for them, they don't know how to react. God is always working in our lives—and His work involves transformation.

People are taught that God wants them to be successful, and that this means they can always expect "the good life." This theology, however, has produced believers who cannot handle change. Instead of being taught the permanency of God's nature and character, they have been taught that God promises the permanency of *things*.

God never guarantees that there won't be times when we'll have to hold on to His promises no matter what things appear to be and against all odds. In the Scriptures, people who were called by God to further His purposes and gain His blessings often lost things before they received something better.

The changes and transitions that come our way are part of the process, and we must hold firmly to God's nature and purposes in the midst of them so that we can arrive safely at the destination He intends. Many people have forfeited their rewards because they've questioned God's love or even their own faith.

We need to learn God's purposes for us, ask Him to guide us, and discern what is next. Then, we will not become overwhelmed by the present on our way to the future. To us, life is unpredictable. To God, life is always moving toward the fulfillment of His ultimate purposes.

*I*t's not only the "good" things in life that are temporary or seasonal. Whatever difficulty you are going through is also only for a season. Whatever is happening to you will not last.

$\mathcal{D}$o you perceive the new things God is doing in your life? Stay in touch with Him through prayer and reading His Word so you won't become overwhelmed by change in your life. Trust Him as your *"strong tower"* (Psalm 61:3) and your *"rock"* (Psalm 18:2).

*Y*ou may experience a time when there are so many changes in your life that you begin to wonder, *Is God against me?* This is the time to remember that He allows change to come in order to fulfill His purposes in us and through us.

I will send down showers in season; there will be showers of blessing" (Ezekiel 34:26). "Showers of blessing" come in seasons. When the blessings start coming, that is not necessarily a permanent condition. When the showers stop, will your faith remain intact? We may think God has forgotten us, but we're only experiencing a season.

There will be particular seasons that bring forth fruit. You may be working hard but not seeing any results. That's just a normal part of the season. You will bring forth your fruit in its time.

$\mathcal{L}$eaves are a sign that a tree is healthy enough to bear fruit. If your life is manifesting "leaves," it means your "roots," or your faith, are still grounded. This is the time to trust God, plan hard, and work diligently. A season will come when you can "feed" others through the fruit you bear.

$\mathcal{R}$ecognizing that God-ordained seasons cannot be resisted or usurped by human will is vital to our response to them. The power that propels these seasons is beyond our comprehension. Even though God has created each of us with a free will, we are still subject to His sovereign purposes for the world.

No matter what our personal desires, wishes, or attitudes may be, we cannot control an unfolding season of divine destiny. The beginning and ending of such a season are not determined by man but by God's sovereign agenda.

There is a providential order in the generational progression of humankind. Understanding the principles and benefits of change, especially in relation to seasons and times, is critical if we are to interpret the activities of God in our generation.

We should be committed to fulfilling our own God-given assignments in our generations. We will receive our rewards as we are faithful to follow His purposes in our changing times.

$\mathcal{G}$od does not *cause* evil. Rather, He *uses* all things—both the good and the bad—for the purpose of moving the world toward His ultimate intent.

A historic convergence is a period of history when major events occur, bringing with them momentous transformations in social, economic, political, and spiritual conditions. Transitional tides incorporate trends that have been building for some time and are bringing about a significant transformation to the world.

The plans of the Lord stand firm forever, the purposes of his heart through all generations" (Psalm 33:11). *"All generations"* would include all changes and transitional tides in human history.

God is in charge of the universe. If He wants to create a new tide in the flow of human history, He will. If He decides to change the leadership of a nation, He will. What the Bible says about change is more important than what the news broadcasts are saying.

Ten defining areas of life are currently converging to bring about a transitional tide in human history. The times in which we're living may be summarized as the age of globalization, information, communication, mobilization, cultural diversification, mergers and networking, longevity of life, technology, political and religious transition, and rapid transformation.

$\mathcal{E}$ven in the midst of change, trust God to work in and through you. *"God has not given us a spirit of fear, but of power and of love and of a sound mind"* (2 Timothy 1:7 NKJV). He will give us strength and wisdom for all the changes we experience in our world.

$\mathcal{W}$e must understand the changes taking place in our world and meet them effectively, or the forces of transition will pull us along and we will have no influence in the midst of them. God will enable *us* to be world changers in the midst of our changing world.

*A*re you comfortable interacting with other cultures? How much do you know about groups of people who are different from you—whether in your own nation or in another nation? As you seek to be part of God's purposes for the world today, will you ignore or accept the reality of cultural change?

*A*n understanding of cross-cultural issues and methods is vital. Those who refuse to venture into, explore, and learn about other nations and the ways of life of their citizens will be culturally illiterate in the twenty-first century and will likely experience eventual culture shock.

Keys for Change

Living in an age of cultural diversity means giving up a fear of other nations and ethnic groups, becoming informed and knowledgeable about them, and being willing to bridge cultural differences for the sake of effective communication, expressing the love of God to others, and sharing the gospel.

The mandate of the church has always been multinational and multicultural in scope. The twenty-first-century church, therefore, requires a multinational, interracial, trans-generational approach that transcends any particular nation's social or political agenda.

A good response to religious change in the world and in our societies is to be sure that our own beliefs and values are strong enough to withstand interaction with cultures that are different from ours.

Sweeping change is exciting to some people. For others, such change threatens their mental and emotional equilibriums. We have to acknowledge transitional tides of change and deal with them instead of allowing the tides to rise over our heads and drown us.

*W*e can initiate change only by
moving into the future.

The steps of a good man are ordered by the Lord" (Psalm 37:23 NKJV). If you are walking in God's will to the best of your ability, then no matter what changes take place, He has you covered.

Why does God position us in various places in life? God positions us to influence others, to change the course of events, and to protect His purposes. This is why one of the most important things you must do is to discover your position in life. What were you born to do?

*P*salm 138:8 says, *"The L*ORD *will fulfill his purpose for me."* No outside force or circumstance can stop God's destiny for your life. Only you can stop it—by ignoring it, rebelling against it, or giving up on it entirely. God does not want you to miss what He's already guaranteed for you to accomplish.

Keys for Change

$\mathcal{T}$ime is one of the greatest gifts God gave humanity. It provides us the opportunity to put our priorities in order and to establish change in our lives. You can make a decision now to start fulfilling your purpose. You can change your behavior in order to have a different experience.

*E*cclesiastes 3:1 says, *"There is a…season for every activity under heaven."* We have to find out as soon as possible what we're meant to do in life, because it's been given a certain period in which to be accomplished. You don't have forever to fulfill your purpose. There's a season for everything.

You can take things out of season, but they will never work well for you. Seasons bring their own inherent blessings. Continue to discern your seasons as you seek God's direction. When it's your season of harvest, doors will start to open, people will begin helping you, and things that had been difficult will become easy.

God will enable you to fulfill the desires He planned for you before time began—desires He has placed in your heart. Let your purpose take you through the pressures, challenges, and changes of life.

Tradition is the greatest hindrance to the positive changes you desire. By *tradition*, I am not referring to timeless truths. Good judgment and sound principles based on God's Word apply to all times. But doing something simply because "it's always been done that way" merely perpetuates the status quo when innovation may be called for.

When we face unexpected or even anticipated problems in society, change is essentially saying to us, "Invent something to correct me."

When we take established methods and practices for granted, depend on earlier successes, and rely on experience as our best or only teacher, we can be blinded to new possibilities. Those who lead change often have to "overlook" experience in favor of attempting the untried. People who forge new frontiers will be successful through change.

*O*ne way we define greatness is by the amount of positive change a person has created. The One who has influenced the world the most is Jesus Christ. We remember Jesus for the everlasting, redemptive change He brought through His life, death, and resurrection. The amount of positive change He initiated can never be calculated.

*B*ecause most people gravitate to the illusion of security, they think there's a place or a condition they can reach in life where they can stop changing. If this were possible, they would also stop growing, expanding, progressing, moving, and developing.

If a company believes it has *the* formula for success, which never needs to vary, it has sealed its own demise. If a community thinks it has reached a perfect state of governance or growth, it has begun to decline. One of the greatest human temptations is to believe that you have arrived.

The older you are, the more change you should initiate. A desire to keep growing and a willingness to respond to change keeps you a vital, contributing member of the human family. But you'll have to work against the culture: the older people grow, the less change they're encouraged to be involved in.

The average person doesn't lead change—he is led by change. Anyone who leads change will contribute significantly to his or her generation. History is a record of people and events that have changed human life in some way. If you want to leave a mark on history, you must initiate or maximize change.

Change agents blend experience and possibility into a *new* experience. Your capacity to learn how to effectively employ new ways of thinking, to use new tools, and to use old tools in new ways will determine whether you will be an initiator of change or a victim of change.

Change challenges us in many ways, but these can be distilled into one main challenge: a test of maturity. Paul indicated that since God was with him, he could experience trouble, hardship, persecution, famine, nakedness, danger, and sword and still be mature in his response to them. (See Romans 8:31–37.)

*Y*our decision to build your life on the rock rather than the sand does not make you immune to the storm, but it *does* affect the outcome—it does affect how you survive it. (See Matthew 7:24–27.) Your faith does not always repel change. Rather, change *proves* the reality of your faith.

*F*our principles of change and maturity are: (1) change tests who we are and who we claim to be, (2) a person's maturity is measured by his or her response to change, (3) change manifests maturity if it's truly there, and (4) through change, we can *learn* the mature response to unsettling times.

KEYS for CHANGE

Some people mourn for years over what happened, what didn't happen, what could have happened, what they used to do, and how things used to be. Those who are mature look to the future and focus on fulfilling their purposes for living.

Maturity has nothing to do with your age. It has to do with your ability to maintain your balance, perspective, and internal peace in the midst of unexpected chaos. If change debilitates you or disarms your mental faculties so they cannot respond and function in a positive and progressive manner, you can be described as immature.

When change occurs, everyone
else around you may believe it's chaos;
they may think it's danger and destruction.
Yet you can approach it by realizing, *God
promises that all things will work together
for good, so there's something good I
have to look for in this.*

When you experience change in the form of a trial, *"consider it pure joy"* (James 1:2). Why? Not because you're immune to pain or sorrow, but because you *know* something. You know that this trial has come to test your faith, to develop your perseverance, and to make you mature.

$\mathcal{D}$on't allow negative things that occur to make *you* negative. Turn them into something positive and use them as a foundation for your next move. A mature person uses adversity for advancement. Allow change to move you forward in personal maturity, abilities, and skills. Use change in your life as you would discipline.

As we initiate and fulfill our God-given purposes, we become change agents. A change agent (1) is open to listening to God's Holy Spirit, who reveals seasons, (2) studies and understands the times, (3) expands his or her knowledge, and (4) applies wisdom. To initiate positive change, we must apply our knowledge and understanding with good judgment.

Engaging with change begins with mental preparedness: (1) an expectation of the inevitability of change, (2) an assurance of your worth to God, (3) a certainty of the value of your contribution to your generation, (4) a decision to pursue your life vision, and (5) a determination to persevere in that vision.

When you are a change agent in God's purposes, you must never confuse being an agent with being the Author of the change. Ultimately, change is happening *through* you and not *by* you. Your season of change is not about fame or other forms of self-gratification. Let humility, understanding, and sensitivity be trademarks of your leadership.

$\mathcal{P}$ositive change can be hindered when those who have been called to be change agents are afraid to accept that calling. It's natural for feelings of uncertainty and fear to accompany any venture into unknown territory. Embrace your call as a divine obligation, as well as a human responsibility toward your fellow men.

Whatever God calls for, He provides for. God gave you potential, ability, gifts, and talents to manage the responsibilities of a season of transition. After you have discovered your true purpose, rise to the task, knowing that you were designed for this moment. Let your initiation of change transform your fear into faith.

$\mathcal{L}$ife is truly a gift from God.
It's a blessing to be given life, and we
need to handle it thoughtfully and carefully.
We can do this by developing, initiating,
and monitoring a plan for positive change
that will help us to fulfill the Creator's
purposes for our lives.

Our destinations in life are determined by our understanding of the purposes God has for us. Our purposes, then, determine the initiation of change in our lives—including the priorities we set, the practices we nurture, and the daily habits we follow—which ultimately leads to the fulfillment of those purposes.

$\mathcal{B}$eing *called* to a purpose, in itself, does not *prepare* you for that calling. You must put things in order to get ready for it. Every human being is given a free will; therefore, we must make the *decision* to *choose our chosen destinies* and do what is necessary to fulfill them.

Changing your life won't happen on its own. You must make decisions and plan your course. First, answer these questions: (1) Where do I want to go in life? (2) What are the Creator-inspired desires of my own heart? (3) What do I want to achieve—specifically? (4) What is my destination in life? (5) What will it take to get there?

$\mathcal{A}$fter you know what changes you need to make in life to fulfill your purpose and have made a detailed plan to get there, you must monitor your course by remaining in constant communication with the Creator and continually reassessing your decisions and activities according to your plan.

*I*n pursuing your purpose, you have to stay close to God and follow His instructions every day through reading His Word and through prayer. He sees the big picture, and He knows how to help you to avoid the obstacles or storms up ahead.

*I*t takes a quality choice to make an effective change. If you make that quality choice in the beginning and follow through all the way to the end, your desired change will become a reality.

*N*ot all change is improvement. Yet without change, there can be no improvement. If you want to improve, you have to alter something in your life. *You* can determine whether you will initiate change to improve your life or merely allow your circumstances to undermine it.

Change *on purpose* so that you are not pushed by change but propelled by your purpose. Initiate ordered change for the benefit of yourself and your environment, facing times of transition with optimism, energy, and personal involvement.

$\mathcal{S}$even ways to plan and prepare for change are: (1) expand your knowledge base, (2) develop new skills, (3) invest in educational resources, (4) develop associations with new people, (5) reorder your priorities, (6) adjust your expectations, and (7) practice good spiritual habits for a strong relationship with God.

$\mathcal{I}$f you move off course from your purpose, it's important not to become discouraged and convince yourself that "it isn't worth trying anymore." It is vital that you don't *stay* off course but immediately make a course correction to move back in line with your purpose. It is never too late to change.

If we give up on our purposes too soon, we might overlook or prevent the arrival of important vehicles of change in our lives.

Take an honest look at where you are in relation to the purposeful changes you want to make in your life. Have you taken a detour? In our hearts, most of us know exactly what we're doing and where we're headed. We know our daily habits. We can't get away with shortcuts or substitutes.

*A*sk yourself, *Have I been distracted from my course to my preferred future? What or who has taken me off course and kept me there? Why haven't I advanced? Does what I'm doing have eternal value? Am I becoming the person I want to become?* Then, recommit to doing what it takes to fulfill your purpose.

$\mathcal{K}$eys to course correction: (1) review, revise, and reset your life vision, (2) assess your obstacles, (3) learn from the failures of others, (4) commit to good counsel and accountability to others, (5) cut off relationships that are hazardous to you, and (6) look for God's *"way out"* (1 Corinthians 10:13) of every temptation.

KEYS FOR CHANGE

*D*on't let a crisis change your course;
let your *choices* change your course.
Receive all the blessings, possibilities,
and opportunities God wants for you.
The past is history. Today is the
beginning of your future.

*I*t is impossible to lead without change, so change is one of a leader's greatest assets. The very purpose and essence of leadership is to move from the known to the unknown in order to create something better for others. Therefore, leadership is created by, motivated by, sustained by, and exists for *change*.

Study the trends and demands of change. Whoever can read seasons of change and be prepared to act on them will be a leader.

Leaders have a major influence on the conditions and attitudes of others. If a leader seems disoriented or overcome by change, this reaction often spreads to the whole environment of the group or organization. Leaders must respond effectively to change for the sake of those whom they're leading, as well as for their own sakes.

The leader almost always confronts change first. The most important work of leadership, therefore, is the ability to handle constant confrontation with change, as well as to initiate change. Leaders are moving continually. They are taking people *to* change, *through* change, *to* change again.

Change is the incubator of leadership development. Through learning about, experiencing, and analyzing change, leaders discover the nature of change, the potential of change, the necessity of change, the power of change, the impact of change, the hazards of change, the challenges of change, and the benefits of change.

$\mathcal{G}$roups, companies, and countries, like individuals, must engage in campaigns of self-development. Research and development departments in many businesses are designed to ensure continuing innovation and implementation of change for the betterment of the company. In the life of an organization or business, success requires periodic reinvention.

KEYS for CHANGE

A leader is a leader because he or she has visited the future in his or her mind and has returned to the present to take others there. Leaders do not stumble into the future; they *plan* their way there. They help those invested in their visions to embrace change and move toward the desired goal.

A true leader provides the vision of a preferred future, initiates a change of direction, sets a change of pace, and encourages participation in reaching the goal. The leader leads by creating the next step toward the future. He or she develops the process and the programs that produce the changes necessary to move toward the desired end.

Leaders do not panic in an atmosphere of change or chaos. These conditions provide an incentive to inspire the leader by testing his or her resolve, capabilities, potential, creativity, and spiritual reserves. Men and women of courage have the audacity to believe God even in the midst of seemingly impossible situations.

What really matters is not what happens to you but what you do about what happens to you. Change agents seek to interpret changes in their environments from the perspective that all change contains within it opportunities that are beneficial to their purposes and causes. They always seek the good in every situation.

Now is the time for you to take on a new mind-set and a new approach based on the benefits of change. Do what you never imagined was possible: take steps toward your preferred future.

$\mathcal{W}$ith all the challenges that we face, we must gain a God-inspired vision of a positive future—not just for our lives in eternity but also for our lives on earth now.

You can think of yourself in connection with your past failures and the negative experiences you have had, or you can trust God to transform your life and give you a positive future.

Each season brings opportunities that we must make use of whenever we can. *"He who gathers crops in summer is a wise son, but he who sleeps during harvest is a disgraceful son"* (Proverbs 10:5). If you've been reluctant to enter into your season of change, it's time for you to start gathering the harvest.

Taking on new responsibilities in our lives involves stepping out in faith while trusting in God's love and provision for us. If we don't take responsibility, we will remain the same as we always have been. And if we remain the same, we will not fulfill our God-given purposes.

People sometimes reject clear purpose and direction from God if they are afraid of what might happen or don't want to take responsibility for doing their parts. If we don't learn to take responsibility for our seasons, we will suffer for our lack of faith and for our inactivity, and we may cause others to suffer, too.

Sometimes, we hold back from moving into the stream of change God is directing us toward because we doubt our own capabilities. You possess the ability to create, develop, perform, and accomplish the ideas and gifts God has placed within you. He gave you all the potential you need to fulfill your purpose in life.

ABOUT THE AUTHOR

Dr. Myles Munroe is an international motivational speaker, best-selling author, educator, leadership mentor, and consultant for government and business. Traveling extensively throughout the world, Dr. Munroe addresses critical issues affecting the full range of human, social, and spiritual development. The central theme of his message is the transformation of followers into leaders and the maximization of individual potential.

Founder and president of Bahamas Faith Ministries International (BFMI), a multidimensional organization headquartered in Nassau, Bahamas, Dr. Munroe is also the founder and executive producer of a number of radio and television programs aired worldwide. He has a B.A. from Oral Roberts University and an M.A. from the University of Tulsa and has been awarded a number of honorary doctoral degrees.

Dr. Munroe and his wife, Ruth, travel as a team and are involved in teaching seminars together. Both are leaders who minister with sensitive hearts and international vision. They are the proud parents of two college graduates, Charisa and Chairo (Myles Jr.).

THE ISLANDS OF THE
bahamas

For Information on Religious Tourism
e-mail: ljohnson@bahamas.com
1.800.224.3681

www.worship.bahamas.com

These inspirational quotes from best-selling author Dr. Myles Munroe
on leadership, single living, marriage, and prayer can be applied
to your life in powerful and practical ways.

Keys for Leadership: ISBN: 978-1-60374-029-6 • Gift • 160 pages
Keys for Living Single: ISBN: 978-1-60374-032-6 • Gift • 160 pages
Keys for Marriage: ISBN: 978-1-60374-030-2 • Gift • 160 pages
Keys for Prayer: ISBN: 978-1-60374-031-9 • Gift • 160 pages

WHITAKER
HOUSE